The Protestant Reformation

THE BEST ONE-HOUR HISTORY

Robert Freeman

The Best One-Hour History™

Kendall Lane Publishers, Palo Alto, CA

ISBN-13: 978-0-9892502-5-2

Contents

1 Introduction..................................... 1

2 The Context of the Time..................... 3

3 Luther and His Protest 11

4 The Protest Escalates 17

5 The Protestants' Reforms 23

7 The Protest Spreads and
the Church Responds....................... 31

8 The Great Civilizational Tumult........... 37

9 Final Word.................................... 45

10 Timeline..................................... 47

1 Introduction

Reform is a curious word. It has the flavor of "change" about it: re-form. Less often associated with reform is "revolution." Yet, when Martin Luther protested certain practices of the Catholic Church in 1517 and tried to reform them, he unknowingly set off one of the greatest revolutions the world has ever known. Without meaning to (at the beginning, anyway), Luther undermined many of the foundations of Church power. In the process, he unleashed a torrent of cultural conflicts and innovations that would end up, at least indirectly, birthing the modern world.

This book explains how this well-intended monk from a small town in Germany rearranged the architecture of religious power in the Western world. It begins by explaining the context of the time—the year 1500—and the grievance Luther was protesting. It then describes the protest itself and how it escalated. It details the deeper theological issues that lay beneath the protest and their implications for the Catholic Church. It discusses how other protesters took up the cause, even as they changed some of Luther's essential ideas, and how the Catholic Church responded. Finally, it finishes with a reflection on how much the modern Western world owes its essential character to the changes Luther unleashed.

A new concept of salvation—by Faith—lay at the heart of Luther's revolution. It required a complete rethinking of man's relationship with God and an equally complete repudiation of the role of the Church as an intermediary between man and God. As a consequence, it shattered the religious unity that had held Europe together as a single cultural entity for a thousand years. Indeed, if we were to reduce the Reformation to its simplest possible seven-word formulation, it might be this: Salvation by faith shattered European religious unity.

Out of this simple idea—an individual's faith—the old order was shaken to its foundations and the seeds of the modern world were planted. This is that story.

2   The Context of the Time

In the year 1500, Europe was in the throes of enormous change. The feudal system that was synonymous with the Middle Ages was breaking down. An entire "New World" had just been discovered in the Americas while Europeans were beginning to sail around the rest of the world. Guttenberg's recent invention of the printing press had created a rapidly growing population of literate town dwellers, a revolution in itself that greatly aided Luther's protest. All of these events put enormous pressures on the established order. In three particular areas—culture, politics, and religion—changes were afoot that would shatter the Christian unity that had defined Europe since the Fall of Rome.

The Cultural Context

The most important element in the cultural context of the Protestant Reformation was the Renaissance, the "rebirth" of culture that had begun around 1350 A.D. and that changed the way European people viewed the world. The names Leonardo,

Michelangelo, and Raphael signify greatness in art unlike anything the world has ever known. But dramatic advances were also occurring in architecture, sculpture, literature, music, letters and other artistic and intellectual mediums. Collectively, these changes would eventually alter the consciousness of the entire continent.

Beneath these artistic revolutions lay a profound change in the way men viewed themselves and their place in the world. As the Muslims tightened their noose around Constantinople, eventually capturing it in 1453, thousands of Christian clerics, scholars, and artists fled to the safety of Europe. They brought with them the treasures of Ancient Greece that had been preserved in the Byzantine Empire (the former Eastern Roman Empire) but that had been lost to the West after the fall of the Western Empire, centered in Rome. These included manuscripts from the works of the greatest Greek thinkers and two especially important ideas: the role of reason as a process for understanding the world; and the place of man in the world.

Reason, of course, had been central to the entire Greek enterprise. The whole discipline of philosophy depended on the certainty that reality could be known through a systematic process of inquiry. Science, another of Greece's great contributions to the world, was founded on a similar belief: that the universe was lawful and that its laws could be discovered through the process of reason. It was

Greece's supreme gift to the world to have plucked man from the Mythos, where the universe was governed by capricious Gods, and to have installed him, instead, in the Logos, where it was governed by predictable Laws.

The second big idea recovered from Greece was the place of humans in the world. It was in Greece that men had first learned to take responsibility for their own fate. Greek literature—from Homer to Sophocles—showed men increasingly becoming distinct from the Gods, even challenging the Gods. Only in a world where men could control themselves could they ever hope to rule themselves, hence, the Greek invention of democracy. This idea of humans as the central actor in the world came to be known during the Renaissance as "Humanism." It was a radical idea, no less so in 1500 A.D. than it was in 500 B.C.

Reason and Humanism created enormous challenges for the Catholic Church. If it ignored them, it would be left behind in the greatest cultural revolution of the past thousand years. But if it embraced them, its beliefs would become tainted, for reason is the opposite of faith, and man is hardly the equal of God. The Church, however, entranced as it was by secular power, did embrace these two ideas, incorporating them into its fundamental theology. In so doing, it sowed the seeds of its own eventual decline.

The Political Context

There are three essential elements in the political context of the time which conditioned the unfolding and the outcome of the Protestant Reformation. These are the power of the Catholic Church, the fact of the Holy Roman Empire, and two outside conflicts, between the Empire and the French Valois and the Empire and the Ottoman Turks.

First, with regards to the Church, the Roman Emperor Constantine had converted to Christianity in 315 A.D. He married the secular power of the Roman Empire with the spiritual authority of the Christian Church. When Rome fell, in 476 A.D., the Western Empire disappeared but the Church carried on, assuming many of the secular responsibilities that had been borne by the Empire. In fact, in the thousand-year "darkness" that followed the fall of Rome, the Church was almost the only civilizing force in the Western world.

By the 1300s, the Church had become Europe's most powerful institution. Its influence extended into every royal court and every feudal estate, from Stockholm in the north to Gibraltar in the south, from London in the west to Hungary in the east. It wielded power over kings and emperors by its control of the "Seven Sacraments" which it had declared to be sacred and, therefore, key to salvation. These were baptism, confirmation, confession, communion, marriage, ordination (election to priesthood), and extreme unction (last rites). But while the

Sacraments gave the Church enormous power, that same power made it inevitable that the church would become entangled in political conflicts.

Second was the issue of the Holy Roman Empire. On top of a patchwork of almost 400 feudal "principalities" in what is modern-day Germany lay the dynastic Holy Roman Empire of the Hapsburgs. The Catholic Hapsburgs controlled the greatest empire since Rome, with holdings in Spain, Portugal, Belgium, France, Germany, Austria, Hungary, Czechoslovakia, Italy, and the New World. But the German people, and especially German princes, resented both the Hapsburgs and the Church. The Hapsburgs interfered with local political rule and the Church took money in tithes, or required donations.

The result was that the German "nation" (as Luther would later call it) was effectively subordinate to both the Catholic Church and the Empire. This left the German people ripe for any kind of relief or reform, either religious or political. Therefore, when Martin Luther accused the Church of corruption and the Pope of being the Anti-Christ, German princes quickly embraced his story. When he articulated a doctrine making the Church subordinate to the State, they fought for it. Luther's new interpretation provided German princes a political and economic rationale for defying both the Catholic Church and the Imperial Hapsburgs.

Finally, the Empire was being challenged by outside forces and had to placate Protestant-leaning

German princes in order to maintain a unified front against two powerful enemies. The first of these enemies was the Valois dynasty, the dominant power of France. War had broken out between the Spanish Hapsburgs and the French Valois in Italy in 1494. This was the context of Machiavelli's *The Prince*. The Valois tried to recruit renegade German princes to fight against the Hapsburgs. This forced the Hapsburgs to be much more lenient in their handling of the German princes, in fear that they might switch sides in the greatest dynastic struggle of the time.

The other outside force influencing the political scene was the Ottoman Turks. Recall that the Turks had captured Constantinople in 1453 and posed a serious threat to Christian Europe. They had begun assaulting Europe in the Mediterranean and in the Balkans. Charles V, the Hapsburg monarch and Holy Roman Emperor, placed himself and his Empire at the service of the Pope in fighting the infidel Turks. In this, he was largely successful, but it meant that, as with the Valois, he had to go easy on the renegade princes within the empire in order to maintain a united front. This made it easier for Protestantism to gain root in German soil.

The Religious Context

As the Church's secular power waxed, its spiritual integrity waned. In many ways, it had become little more than any other earthly kingdom, contending for power and wealth with the other monarchies of Europe. In three areas in particular, it had abandoned the spiritual discipline that had made it such a powerful organizing force after the fall of Rome.

First, the Church's theology had become watered down as it extended its teachings to stay current with the cultural trends of its time. As noted above, it had incorporated the Greek ideals of reason and Humanism into its basic teachings. It had also accepted the veneration of the saints and the adoration of the Virgin Mary. It had proliferated all manner of rituals and celebrations as devices to both bind the people to its ministrations, but also to raise money from the donations that accompanied them. All of these practices had the effect of weakening central Church teachings.

Second, the Church officiate, from the local priest up to the Pope himself, had become lax and corrupt. The Church ideal held that the clergy should be exemplars of the Christian man: wise; simple; and poor. Instead, the clergy—and certainly the higher officers of Church authority—were often ignorant, clever, and wealthy. Against the Church policy of celibacy, they frequently kept women as concubines. Against their vows of poverty, the officials in Rome lived in decadent opulence, extorting money from parishioners in exchange for a promised easier treatment at Judgment Day. Instead of Christ-like humility they conducted themselves with Caesar-like arrogance. All of these practices had the effect of reducing the moral authority of the Church in the eyes of the people it was supposed to serve.

Finally, the papacy itself had become little more than a vast money making operation. It sold "offices," or church positions, to the highest bidders who could turn around and use them as collection rackets, milking donations from superstitious and fearful parishioners. It allowed bishops to hold multiple offices at the same time, effectively franchising religious-based tax collections. And in the most nefarious operation, the one that would provoke Luther's protest, they sold "Indulgences," grants of the remission of sins based on payments to the Church.

For all of these reasons, then, cultural, political, and religious, the Church's authority, moral stature, and power had fallen greatly in the eyes of Europe's people. All agreed that reform was desperately needed. Indeed, some of the most insistent and authoritative voices for reform issued from within the Church itself, for example from the Dutch churchman Erasmus. His condemnations of Church practices were so biting and persistent it was said of him, "He laid the egg that Luther hatched." The only questions were how reform would begin and what form it would take. The answers came in the second decade of the sixteenth century.

3   Luther and His Protest

There would be no Protestant Reformation without the protests and reforms of Martin Luther. Less obvious is the role Luther's background played in his challenges to the Church. Luther was born and lived in Saxony, part of the Holy Roman Empire. It was at the outer fringes of Christendom, far removed from the intellectual innovations and cultural decadence of Renaissance Rome. Importantly, however, it was an area that had long been a hotbed of theological ferment, going back to the Bohemian heretic Jan Hus, in the early 1400s.

Hus had challenged many doctrines of the Church. He was critical of papal power and proposed that the Church be led by councils of believers, an idea known as "Conciliarism." This was a precursor of Luther's "Priesthood of All Believers." Hus also inveighed against Church corruption, writing, "One pays for confession, for mass, for the sacrament, for indulgences, for churching a woman, for a blessing, for burials, for funeral services, and prayers." Luther, writing a hundred years later, would echo many of

Hus' condemnations. Hus was killed after having been promised safe passage to a Church conclave to defend his ideas.

Luther's personal background was also significant to his protest. He was a sensitive person, wracked with doubt about his worthiness in the eyes of God. He was certain that he was saturated with sin, both "original" and of his own doing, and would be condemned by God to eternal damnation. Caught in a thunderstorm in 1505, he feared for his life and cried out, "Saint Anne protect me. I will become a monk!" He carried out his promise and entered the Dominican order where he began intense study of the Gospels, and even more intense efforts to try to cleanse himself of his perceived sins. It didn't work.

Luther despaired of ever being able to make himself worthy in the eyes of God. So total was man's depravity, he believed, that trying to expiate sins on a case-by-case, sin-by-sin basis was folly. What was needed was a complete head-to-toe reform in man's relation with God. Man had to surrender all pretenses of worthiness and throw himself on God's mercy. He had to have complete faith in God's goodness and in Christ's agency, and resign himself that, come what may, God would deal with him in the way that was Just. This transformation, anchored in faith, would become known as The Doctrine of Salvation by Faith Alone. It is the central pillar of Protestant theology.

The Immediate Provocation

In 1517, Pope Leo X began raising money to complete the building of St. Peter's Basilica in Rome. He sold the office of the Bishop of Mainz in Germany to Prince Albert of Hohenzollern for 10,000 ducats. Albert had borrowed the money and the deal was that he could use the office to sell Indulgences to parishioners. Half the money raised through the sales would go to pay back the loan. The other half would go to the Pope. Albert would retain the Bishopric and all the revenues it generated once the loan was paid off. It was a win-win deal for both Albert and the Pope.

Indulgences were a device invented by earlier popes to collect contributions from parishioners. Luther mockingly called them, "the doctrine of cheap grace." They worked like this: the Pope claimed that earlier saints had possessed more "merits" than had been needed to effect their salvation. The collective excess of all these merits was stored in a "Treasury of Merits" in heaven that the Pope could draw from to remit sins. But people had to pay. The final line of a popular jingle of the time went, "As soon as gold in the basin rings, right then the soul to heaven springs." It was a parody of the Church's tight coupling of Indulgences with money.

Indulgences could be bought to cover almost any sin. Common applications included the sins of lust, pride, marital infidelity, dishonesty in commercial transactions, and so on. Soon, the Pope was remitting sins for people's relatives who were already dead but in purgatory, awaiting Judgment. It was a fantastic, cost-free money-making scheme, all premised on church members' guilt and the claim of the Pope to be able to remit sins. But to Luther, a deeply committed monk, it was the most outrageous of frauds.

The Ninety-Five Theses

In response, Luther wrote what was to become one of the most important documents in the history of the Western world: *Ninety-Five Theses.* The subtitle of the document is, *Disputation on the Power and Efficacy of Indulgences.* On All Saints Day (today's Halloween), 1517, Luther nailed the document to the door of Wittenberg cathedral in Germany inviting anyone to debate the issue with him, either in person or by letter. In *Ninety Five Theses,* Luther laid out his objections to Indulgences.

First, said Luther, the practice itself was tawdry, inviting disrespect by all who knew of it. In Thesis 66, Luther sneered, "Indulgences are the nets with which the Church fishes for rich men." Second, there was no such thing as a Treasury of Merits, according to Luther. Since salvation was a gift from God and God alone, any "merits" associated with it were God's and not a dispensation that could be issued by the Pope in exchange for money.

Third, even if such excesses of merits had existed, it was not in the Pope's power to remit sins. It was only in God's. In Thesis 33, Luther stated, "Men must be on their guard against those who say that the Pope's pardons are that inestimable gift of God by which man is reconciled to Him." And in Thesis 34, he follows, saying, "For these 'graces of pardon' concern only the penalties appointed by man." Fourth, Luther mocked the Pope's claim to have jurisdiction over purgatory, stating in Thesis 82: "Why does not the Pope empty purgatory, for the sake of holy love and of the dire need of the souls that are there?"

Most importantly, however, Indulgences induced the wrong state of mind on the part of the sinner, said Luther. Rather than an attitude of contrition, they promoted bargaining and negotiation—hardly the states of mind calculated to promote repentance. In Thesis 49 Luther stated, "Christians are to be taught that the Pope's pardons are harmful, if through them they lose their fear of God." In other words, if a sinner believed he could simply buy his way out of Judgment through the purchase of an Indulgence, there was little likelihood he would fundamentally change his behavior. Indulgences, therefore, only served to seduce already weak men into ever more spiritually dangerous and destructive behavior. They were the exact opposite of what the Church should be doing for its flock.

In addition to condemning Indulgences, Luther also used the Ninety-Five Theses to reiterate the essential teachings of the Bible regarding proper

Christian conduct. In Thesis 43, he wrote, "Christians are to be taught that he who gives to the poor or lends to the needy does a better work than buying pardons." And in Thesis 45, "Christians are to be taught that he who sees a man in need, and passes him by, and gives his money for pardons, purchases not the Indulgences of the Pope, but the indignation of God." In Thesis 94, "Christians are to be exhorted that they be diligent in following Christ, their Head, through penalties, deaths, and hell." Luther concludes in the 95th Thesis: "And thus be confident of entering into heaven through many tribulations, rather than through the assurance of peace."

Luther had intended that his *Theses* be the subject of monastic debate. Nailing them to the cathedral door was simply the conventional way to invite such debate. But the document was printed in nearby Nuremberg and distributed widely throughout Saxony. That is when a narrow academic issue of the efficacy of a Church practice ballooned into the public controversy that it ultimately became.

4 The Protest Escalates

lmost immediately, the matter exploded beyond the issue of Indulgences to a question of Church authority. Luther was a fairly low-level monk in a somewhat remote part of Christendom — far away from the high-minded theological center of Rome. The question, therefore, became: who has the authority to speak for the Church, and therefore, for God? The Church's position was clear: if the Pope had declared Indulgences to be spiritually sound, then that settled the matter. The monk from Wittenberg must retract his claims and submit to papal authority. But Luther would not recant. Instead, he stepped up his attack.

The original *Ninety-Five Theses* had focused only on Indulgences. Luther now went after the doctrine of papal authority — the idea that the Pope must be obeyed, no matter what. The Pope replied by charging Luther with heresy, the sustained and open opposition to Church authority, and by ordering him silenced. But Luther was protected by both the rector of the Wittenberg monastery and by the local prince,

Frederick the Wise. The political tensions between Germany and Rome were beginning to come into play.

In 1520, Luther was ordered to Rome to explain himself to the Council of Cardinals. Instead, he published two of the most incendiary documents of the entire affair. In his *Open Letter to the Christian Nobility of the German Nation*, he urged German princes to reject the authority of the Church in Rome. To convey just how inflammatory the document was, it is necessary to quote it at some length:

> "It is a horrible and frightful thing that the ruler of Christendom [the Pope], who boasts himself vicar of Christ, lives in such worldly splendor that no king or emperor can equal or approach him...
>
> They have maintained that the Pope is above the angels in heaven and has authority over them. These are indeed the very words of the Antichrist...
>
> Italy and Germany have many rich monasteries and beneficences. No better way has been discovered to bring all these to Rome than by creating cardinals and giving them the bishoprics, monasteries and prelacies...No Turk could have so devastated Italy and suppressed the worship of God...
>
> Now that Italy is sucked dry, they come into Germany. But let us beware, or Germany will soon become like Italy...Antichrist must

take the treasures of the earth, as it was prophesied...

How comes it that we Germans must put up with such robbery and such extortion of our property, at the hands of the Pope...Why do we Germans let them make such fools and apes of us?

The German princes should consider that they, too, are Christians, and should protect their people against these ravening wolves who, in sheep's clothing, pretend to be shepherds...they should not permit their land and people to be so sadly robbed and ruined, against all justice..."

Instead of secular subordination to the Church, Luther argued that it should be the other way around: the Church should be placed beneath the authority of the local prince, reflecting Jesus' admonition to "Render unto Caesar that which is Caesar's, and render unto God that which is God's." Each prince should be able to choose what religion would be practiced in his own domains. The local nobility, looking for a justification for greater independence, liked this idea and supported Luther, not only against Rome, but against the Catholic Hapsburg Empire as well.

Later in 1520, Luther published *The Babylonian Captivity of the Church*, in which he claimed that the Catholic Church had been highjacked by a cabal of Antichrists who kept control of Christendom by domination of the Sacraments. He denied the legitimacy of all the Sacraments except baptism and communion, the two that actually appeared in the New Testament. But, he declared the doctrine of transubstantiation, where the priest is purported to turn bread and wine into the body and blood of Christ, was "magic," a provocative reference to medieval paganism. This was a frontal assault on the legitimacy of the Church's central practice. Upon reading the work, Erasmus declared, "The breach is irreparable!" And, indeed, it was.

Following publication of these tracts, Luther was commanded to appear before the Imperial Diet at Worms to explain himself and to recant his words. He was given several days to consider and reconsider his actions, but in the end he stood by them. His testimony was one of most singular statements of conscience and individualism in the Western world. As with the *Open Letter*, above, it is worth quoting at some length:

> "Your Imperial Majesty and Your Lordships…I cannot provide my writings with any other defense than that which my Lord Jesus Christ provided for His teaching. When He had been interrogated concerning His teaching He said: "If I have spoken evil, bear witness of the evil…"
>
> I seek and wait for any who may wish to bear witness against my teaching, to defeat

them by the writings of the Prophets or by the Gospels; for I shall be most ready, if I be better instructed, to recant any error...

You demand a simple answer. Here it is, plain and unvarnished. Unless I am convinced of error by the testimony of Scripture...my conscience is taken captive by God's word. I cannot and will not recant anything, for to act against our conscience is neither safe for us, nor open to us.

On this I take my stand. I can do no other. So help me God. Amen."

Luther was excommunicated, kicked out of the Church and condemned as an apostate, one who has renounced Church teachings. However, he continued his crusade, the "Protest" after which his new form of Christianity would eventually be named. In 1522, he published the first-ever version of the New Testament in the German language. This was itself an explosive event. Due to the invention of printing by Guttenberg in Germany only a few decades before, the German people were the most literate in the world. They could read for themselves that many of the claims for spiritual authority made by the Catholic Church, including five of the seven Sacraments and the position of the Pope himself, were not mentioned anywhere in the Bible.

In 1526, Luther wrote a German language version of the mass where the parishioners actually received the bread and wine of communion. In 1534, he published a German translation of the Old Testament. He involved the Christian masses in hymns, Bible teachings, and youth practices, all in German. Indeed, Luther repudiated the role of the clerical priesthood — another assault on the Church — and declared that the people themselves constituted a "priesthood of all believers." In all these ways, Luther "democratized" Christianity, making it accessible to all people. Luther died in 1546.

5   The Protestants' Reforms

Indulgences and challenges to papal authority are conspicuous at the start of the Protestant Reformation, but they are, in fact, only "proximate" causes — the spark that ignited a keg of gunpowder that was already ready to blow. At its heart, the Reformation was a revolution in theology — in man's understanding of God. Simply put, said Luther, the Catholic Church had become infected with paganism through its association with Renaissance Humanism, and it had erred in its essential understanding of the nature of God. As a result, it had betrayed its fundamental duty: to act as worthy shepherds for men's souls.

Fundamental Theological Issues

Luther believed that the medieval synthesis of the Catholic saint, Thomas Aquinas, was deeply, indeed, irretrievably, flawed. Aquinas' great work, *Summa Theologica*, had created an amalgam of Christian theology and Greek philosophy, the latter based on the teachings of Aristotle. It was the Church's attempt to assimilate the Greek influence coming to Europe even before the Renaissance by accommodating reason as one of the ways of knowing the world and, therefore, God. But to Luther, this was sacrilege bordering on idolatry.

In Luther's view, God was so far above man, He was unknowable, by reason or any other method. Attempting to "know" or "understand" God through exercises of reason was like a beetle trying to "know" or "understand" man by wiggling its antennae. It was doomed by its nature and delusional in its pretense. Even trying it was dangerous because it only seduced men into the folly of arrogance and, therefore, damnation.

Still worse, believed Luther, the Church's very idea of God himself was flawed. It had been crafted by the late-Roman-era theologian, Saint Augustine, in the early fifth century near the time of the Fall of Rome. Augustine had taken the teachings of Saint Paul and blended them with the cosmology of Plato. It was Plato's fourth century B.C.E. concepts of the "Ideal Realm" and the "Material Realm" that became the Christian concepts of the Kingdom of Heaven and the Kingdom of Earth. Indeed, the very idea of Jesus can be understood as the Material expression (man) of an Ideal entity (God). Augustine's Christianity was indelibly Platonic: a universe where the ideal God suffuses all of existence with his manifest nature.

But this idea of God-with-man-not-so-distant was heresy to Luther. In Luther's mind, God was as fundamentally different from man as men are from worms. Attempts to narrow the chasm that separated them by having men work their way toward God with reason or good works were an affront to God himself. If man would only have faith in God's infinite grace, he might—might—have a chance for salvation. But it wasn't in the hands of man. No amount of propitiation, no amount of good works or appeasement, certainly nothing as tawdry as an Indulgence, could change God's decision about man's salvation.

In other words, Luther wanted to return to a more simple time when people practiced a more simple, "authentic" Christianity. He wanted to go back before Aquinas had brought in Aristotle, even before Augustine and his indirect embrace of Plato. Luther wanted Christianity to go back to the God of Paul, a God who was infinitely powerful, remote, and above all, judgmental. It was the God of the Jews from whom Paul had emerged. It was the God of Christianity before the conversion of Constantine had corrupted the Church with the secular entanglements of Empire. And most importantly, it was the God of Jesus before it had become defiled by the pagan teachings of Greece. Luther was a reactionary, someone who wanted to return to what he imagined to have been a "golden age." He was the original Christian fundamentalist.

Secondary Theological Issues

Once Luther's understanding of the nature of God was accepted, it followed that many of the secondary teachings of Christian doctrine also came into question. The three most important of these secondary issues were the ideas of Justification, Predestination, and Scripture as the source of religious authority.

First, according to Luther, Justification (salvation) was accomplished only by the act of faith on the part of the believer, and even then only through the grace of God. It was NOT in man's control. Luther's authority for this doctrine was, among others, a passage from the New Testament, Ephesians 2:8-9:

"By Grace are ye saved, and by Faith. And even that is not of yourself but comes as a gift of God; not of works, lest any man should boast."

In other words, salvation could not be achieved by donating money to the church, by buying Indulgences, or by any other "good works." Rather, only the believer's faith in Jesus Christ would serve to make him worthy of heaven. And even then, it was still up to God whether or not a sinful person would ever be admitted.

This "Doctrine of Salvation by Faith Alone," as it came to be known, led to a second important implication: Predestination. According to Luther, since salvation was wholly a matter of God's will, man could do nothing to effect his own ultimate fate. It was entirely in the hands of God. Notice how different this is from the Greek idea of fate where men play a role in their own destiny, and the Church's idea of "good works" where a person's donations can bear on his chances of salvation. Here, man's will, his thoughts, his actions, were all immaterial in deciding his final destiny. Predestination became one of the cornerstones of Lutheran theology.

Finally, Luther believed that the only certain source of religious knowledge was Scripture itself. Only by reading the Bible could the Christian believer come to an understanding of God. There was no place for interpretation by popes or priests. This doctrine became known as "Sola Scriptura." It would produce masses of Bible-reading Christians, Luther's "priesthood of all believers." It was to have major implications for the legitimacy of Catholic teachings and in leveling the hierarchy that was implicit in the Catholic Church.

Practical Implications

These three secondary theological issues produced three direct, corresponding attacks on the Church. First, Justification by Faith called into question the efficacy of the Sacraments. If a person's salvation was a matter only of faith (and God's will), then Sacraments were useless, simply mystical devices made up by the Church to keep parishioners in thrall to ritual. Luther pared back the Sacraments from seven to two, retaining only those that were recorded in the Gospels: baptism and communion. This denunciation of the Sacraments directly attacked the foundation of the Church's power: its ability to improve a man's chances of getting into heaven.

Second, Predestination attacked the foundation of Church finances. If a person's fate was already predetermined by God, there was no use in donating money to the Church. The idea of tithing—giving a percentage of your money to the Church—was meaningless. Similarly, "good works," such as donating money for building cathedrals, were equally useless. Indulgences, one of the Church's biggest money makers, were positively evil for reasons discussed above. In all of these ways, then, Predestination undercut the need for the Christian believer to give money to the Church.

Finally, Luther's insistence that the only true source of religious knowledge came from Scripture attacked the role of the Church as an intermediary between man and God. This is what Luther intended. The Church had maintained that it had special access to God through the Pope, whom it called "Christ's Vicar on Earth." Luther charged that this was a fraud. Man could only know God's will by reading the Scriptures and adopting the proper attitude of spirit. The Catholic Church interfered with a man's direct communion with God and, therefore, was evil.

Thus, Luther's teachings undermined the foundations of the Church's power, its finances, and its claim to legitimacy. Luther had started out merely hoping to reform Church teachings regarding Indulgences. But before it was over, his Reformation had escalated into a life-and-death challenge to the very existence of the Church itself. It is easy to see why his actions ignited such intense, widespread, and long-lasting opposition.

The two sides to the conflict did attempt to bridge their differences. At the Colloquy of Regensburg in 1541, emissaries came together to consider issues of original sin, free will, predestination, and the Sacraments. Though there was some agreement between them, a full reconciliation was rejected by both Luther and the Pope. The Peace of Augsburg, negotiated in 1555 by the Empire and the German princes, gave legal recognition to Protestantism within the Holy Roman Empire. The formulation was "cuius regio, eius religio" or "who rules, his religion." It allowed each prince to determine the religion that would be practiced in his domain. It was the first formal, legal acceptance of Protestantism in the Western world.

7   The Protest Spreads and the Church Responds

In the Catholic Church, there is only one interpretation of Christianity and the authority on all matters is the Pope. But in Luther's Christianity, every person is a priest. Every person talks to God directly. As a result, there quickly emerged many different — sometimes competing — interpretations of what it meant to be a Christian. These alternate visions ultimately became the kaleidoscope of sects that today make up the Protestant faiths: Lutheran; Methodist; Episcopalian; Baptist; Presbyterian; Mormon; Congregationalist; Quaker; Mennonite; Unitarian; and so on.

Other Leading Protesters

The first of the alternatives to Luther's vision came from the Swiss theologian, Ulrich Zwingli. Though trained as a Catholic priest like Luther, Zwingli was much more a Humanist than Luther was. He maintained a correspondence with Erasmus before Luther wrote *Ninety-Five Theses*. Like Luther, he denied the authority of the Pope in matters of religious interpretation, relying, as Luther did, only on scripture. Also like Luther, he was against what he called "superstitious elements" of Church practice including Indulgences. But Zwingli differed from Luther in several important matters and these differences presaged the fracturing of Protestant unity that would ultimately become its hallmark.

Zwingli differed with Luther on the question of Predestination, believing that men had free will with which they could affect their chances for salvation. Without free will, argued Zwingli, there would be no capacity, and therefore no incentive, for men to make moral choices. This was a point of theological contention within the Church itself, and very much in keeping with Zwingli's Humanist background.

Zwingli also differed with Luther on communion. Recall that the Catholic Church taught that during the act of communion the priest turned bread and wine into body and blood. Luther disputed this, but believed that the "Real Presence" of Jesus would be summoned in the act. Zwingli went even further in desacralizing the ceremony, teaching that it was only symbolic of Christ's sacrifice. This caused him to become alienated from Luther—the first of many "schisms" to afflict Protestantism.

Finally, Luther believed the church should be beneath the secular authority of the state, the better to avoid temptations among its members to secular power. Zwingli believed society should be a theocracy, that church and state should be indistinguishable—the same institution. Zwingli died in 1531 leading Zurich in a battle with Swiss Catholic cantons.

If Zwingli was the earliest innovator after Luther, surely the most consequential was John Calvin. Calvin was a French lawyer living in Switzerland who used his knowledge of the law to build a model for church governance that would ultimately have as much influence on Protestantism as Luther's theological teachings had. His *Institutes of the Christian Religion*, first published in 1536, was something of a Protestant *Summa* in that it derived a complete theology from simple initial premises.

But it went further than Aquinas' work had, using political theory to meld church organization with Biblical principles. It prescribed rules and procedures for how to run a Protestant church, maintain the purity of practices, train the clergy, educate the laity, and much more. It became the "operating manual" for most Protestant churches founded over the following century. In this way, while Luther's contribution was the impetus that started Protestantism, it was Calvin's that made possible its wide-spread propagation.

Calvin's theology differed from Luther's (and Zwingli's) in important ways. He believed church and state should be separate but co-equal, an approach that made it easy to adapt to new political settings. His idea of communion lay somewhere between Luther's near-literalism and Zwingli's sparse symbolism—that the Real Presence occurred *provided* the practitioner had true faith, but not if he did not. He outdid Luther on free will, claiming "double Predestination," where "both the elect and the reprobate, the saved and the damned" had been chosen in advance by God.

It was Calvin's form of Protestantism that spread the most widely throughout northern Europe and to America. Calvin believed that the sign of a person having been "chosen" by God was outward moral behavior. This led to ostentatious displays of moral uprightness, for example, the austere and extreme moralism that characterized the early American settlers: the Pilgrims. The French Huguenots who rebelled against the Catholic monarchy in the late sixteenth century were Calvinists. So, too, were the Dutch who rebelled against and ultimately won national liberation from the empire of Catholic Spain. The Puritans of England who overthrew and killed their king in the mid-1600s were likewise practicing a variant of Calvinism.

The Church Responds

Protestantism spread quickly and far, especially through the countries of northern Europe. But it was fiercely resisted by the Catholic Church whose authority, wealth, and standing in the courts of Europe were at risk. As a result, the Church mounted a vigorous defense and partial reform of its practices, and an aggressive attack on Protestantism. The defense and reform became known as the Catholic Reformation, while the attack was called the Counter-Reformation.

The most important force in the Catholic Reformation was the Council of Trent. It was convened in 1545 in the Italian city of Trent to review the doctrines and practices of the Church in order to make the Church more resilient against the appeal of Protestantism. The Council was very conservative, affirming almost all of the historical Catholic practices, including the Sacraments, Indulgences, good works, and veneration of the saints. It affirmed the theology of Aquinas with its optimistic view of man as against that of Augustine and Luther and their more pessimistic view.

The Council of Trent did reform many of the more offensive Church practices. Priests were required to be more educated. Concubinage was forbidden. Priests had to be in residence at their parishes. Offices could not be sold and the plurality of offices was greatly reduced. More money was dedicated to relieving the poverty of church members. But the reforms were too little, too late. Protestantism had taken root and could not be undone. While the reforms of Trent revived Church discipline and slowed the advance of Protestantism in Europe, they could not reverse it.

In order to try to eradicate Protestantism, the Church launched the Counter-Reformation. Its nominal goal was to reclaim the souls that had been lost to Protestantism. In practice, this meant rolling back Protestantism, even if that meant having to hunt down and kill heretics. The Roman Inquisition was initiated in 1542, partly in emulation of what was considered the success of the earlier Spanish Inquisition which had been used to purge Spain of Muslims and Jews. Someone accused by the Inquisition was assumed guilty until he could prove his innocence. An Index of Prohibited Books was published by the Church in 1559, in recognition of the effectiveness that pamphleteering had enjoyed in furthering the spread of Protestantism. A person caught with a Prohibited Book could be deprived of property or even killed.

One of the most visible initiatives of the Counter-Reformation was the establishment of the Society of Jesus, or Jesuit order. The Spanish monk, Ignatius Loyola, founded the order in the 1530s. It became one of the most aggressive of Catholic orders, carrying Catholicism to the Far East and to Latin America. Loyola himself had experienced an emotional conversion much as Luther had, and he possessed the pragmatic organizing skills of Calvin. The Jesuits prescribed intense religious discipline and loyalty to the Pope and focused on education of young males from rich families as a way to increase recruitment to the Catholic Church.

8 The Great Civilizational Tumult

One of the most dramatic — certainly the most violent — outcomes of the Protestant Reformation was the hundred-and-thirty years of wars (1517 – 1648) that followed Luther's posting of *Ninety-Five Theses*. These wars involved all of the nations of Europe and all of the confessional faiths. They greatly diminished the power and influence of the Catholic Church. The wars left Europe so deeply scarred that when the Americans were designing their own government in the late 1700s, the Founding Fathers wanted to keep religion and politics as far away from each other as possible. So, they included (according to Thomas Jefferson) the idea of "separation of church and state" in the First Amendment of the Bill of Rights.

A Century of War

The Dutch Revolt was one of the earliest of these wars. It lasted from 1556 to 1648. The Spanish Hapsburgs owned what we know today as the

Netherlands. But the northern Netherlands had adopted Calvinism. Their people were models of Protestant piety and Calvinist industry—serious, modest, thrifty, disciplined, and sober. When the Hapsburg King Phillip II tried to enforce his Catholic practices on the Protestant Dutch in 1556, rebellion broke out. Phillip dispatched an army and began killing thousands of Dutch protesters.

But oppression only strengthened the resistance, at first on religious, but later on nationalist grounds. The fighting lasted for almost a century, until 1648, when it was finally settled at the Peace of Westphalia. The northern Netherlands remained Protestant and became Holland while the southern provinces continued their Catholic practice and became modern day Belgium. The Dutch Revolt itself was cited by the Spanish foreign minister as the single biggest cause for the fall of the Spanish Empire.

The French Wars of Religion were a French civil war in the late sixteenth century. The Wars began in 1562 and continued through the reign of four different French kings. Catholic France had been inundated by Calvinists from neighboring Switzerland. Calvinism was especially attractive to French noblemen who, like their German counterparts, used the guise of religion to give cover to their political conflicts with the ruling monarchy. The Wars were uniquely savage for their day with many tens of thousands—mainly Protestants—killed for their religious beliefs.

The Wars involved the leading dynasties of France including the Valois, the Guise, the Montmorency, and the Bourbon families. King Phillip II of Spain joined the side of the Catholics while Elizabeth I of England supported the Protestants. The Edict of Nantes put to rest the religious conflict in 1598. It was similar to the Peace of Augsburg of 1555 which had created religious toleration within Germany. The winner of the Wars was Henry IV of the Bourbon family, which began a dynastic rule that would continue until the French Revolution in 1789. The real loser in the Wars was Spain, which saw a greatly strengthened French government emerge from the conflict. However, the expansion of Protestantism was halted in France, which still today remains a predominantly Catholic country.

The Thirty Years War began in 1618. It bears the dubious honor of being the bloodiest war in the history of the world up until that time. The War started in Bohemia in what is the modern-day Czech Republic as a dispute between the Protestant King and the Catholic Emperor. It quickly spread to almost all of the German speaking territories of northern Europe. Protestant Sweden, fearing a Catholic Hapsburg victory, entered the fight in 1630. France, though Catholic, also feared a strengthened Hapsburg monarchy, so entered on the side of the Protestant princes. This is the tip-off that the War, which had begun as a religious conflict, had become a dynastic struggle between the major powers of Europe.

The War was finally ended by the Peace of Westphalia in 1648, one of the landmarks in international law. The settlement defined for the first time the basic concept of the nation state: that a ruler is sovereign within recognized international boundaries. And by enlisting all of the states of Europe into the settlement, it began the practice of international law. The War proved a grievous blow to Spain but, like the French Wars of Religion, greatly consolidated the strength of the French monarchy.

Finally, the English Civil Wars lasted from 1642 to 1648 but their seeds were planted more than a century earlier when, in 1535, Henry VIII broke with the Catholic Church to found the Anglican Church of England with himself as its head. Henry's daughter, Elizabeth produced no heirs, so James I of the Catholic Stuart family ascended to the throne. James' son, Charles I, started the Civil Wars by trying to foist a crypto-Catholic prayer book on Protestant Scotland.

Charles was opposed in the Wars by the Scottish Puritan, Oliver Cromwell. Charles lost the Wars and was beheaded in 1649, the first time in over a thousand years that a sitting monarch had been killed by his own people. Charles' son, James II fought with Parliament over religious oaths for government offices. Parliament finally tired of James' Catholic machinations and chased him out of the country in 1689. They replaced him with the Protestant king of Holland, William of Orange, and his wife Mary. This "Glorious Revolution" officially enshrined Protestantism into the succession of the English monarchy and signaled the beginning of the ascendancy of parliamentarianism over monarchy.

The Deep Origins of the Modern Western World

The Protestant Reformation was revolutionary far beyond the immediate realm of religion. Its effects spilled over into culture, politics, economics, and even man's relationship with the physical world. The religious egg that was laid by Luther's Protest hatched as the uniquely Western institutions of individualism, the nation state, capitalism, and science. To the extent that these are defining characteristics of the modern world, the Protestant Reformation may properly be seen as one of that world's most important progenitors.

Individualism had arisen as a Western ideal in Greece but had been lost during the Middle Ages. Protestantism, together with the Humanism of the Renaissance, revived the idea. In Protestantism, the locus for religious knowledge is not the Church, the pope, or tradition, but the individual and his own understanding of scripture. A person's soul is saved not by Sacraments, Indulgences, or good works, but by his own singular faith. In this way, the individual became more important than any clergy member, indeed, more important than even nobles or kings, for the individual had access to eternal salvation whereas nobles and kings only had recourse to the baubles of the material world.

The nation state was also greatly strengthened by the Protestant Reformation. First, of course, was Luther's assertion that the church should be subordinate to the state. This reversed over 800 years of Church teaching, which had held that the Church, as the agent of God, was superior to any earthly institution. The wars that followed Luther's revolt also increased the power of the national state, especially in France, England, and the Netherlands. The tension between church and state became so great in the centuries after Luther, their separation became a central issue in defining the character of America. As mentioned above, it was enshrined in the First Amendment to the U.S. Constitution.

Capitalism was another important — although indirect — beneficiary of Protestantism. Protestantism cultivated a certain character in it adherents that was distinct from that cultivated under Catholicism. Protestants, especially Calvinists, were taught to be innovative, industrious, sober, and thrifty, the better to build visible evidence of their worthiness in the eyes of God. Then, since they had no need for "good works" (since salvation was preordained by God), they had no reason to give money to the Church. The result was that the excess fruits of their hard work accumulated as "capital" in their businesses and became the powerful foundation of a new economic order, the one that overturned medieval feudalism.

Finally, science arose indirectly from the Protestant Reformation. Under Luther's "Reforms," the world became disentangled from the divine essence of Plato and the first causes of Aristotle. The result was that the world was no longer divine and unknowable, but rather, was mundane and knowable precisely because it wasn't saturated with God. And with men now having the power of discovering truths for themselves, they broke their dependency on authority for knowledge. The result was that, just as men consulted the scriptures and used faith to understand the spiritual world, they could now consult evidence and use reason to understand the physical world. These two changes — a mundane world distinct from God, and men empowered to discover truths for themselves — soon led to the invention of science. It is not an accident that those nations that most embraced Protestantism — England, Sweden, Germany, The Netherlands, and Denmark — led the way in the development of science as well.

9 Final Word

If Augustine was the great Catholic theologian who ushered in the Middle Ages with his articulation of Christian orthodoxy at the time of the Fall of Rome, it was Luther, the great Catholic reformer, who ushered them out by causing a second "Fall of Rome." It is the ironies that follow Luther's Protest that signal just how revolutionary the Reformation really was.

Luther sought to reduce the role of reason in religion, replacing it with faith, but instead, helped elevate reason to the highest position in science, which then replaced religion as the way Europeans came to know the world. He wanted to cleanse Christianity of the pagan-tainted Humanism of the Renaissance and, instead, made the individual the central actor in the Western world. He deplored the crass materialism of the Pope, yet inadvertently accelerated the rise of capitalism. And in trying to extricate the Church from the secular entanglements of empire, he boosted the power and fortunes of the nation state which would soon displace the Church as the dominant organizing institution of the modern world.

Luther's influence on the founding of America is especially poignant. His challenge to the Church made him the supreme cultural model for confronting authority — the basis of the American revolution, which, or course, was carried out by Protestant colonists. When he nailed the *Ninety-Five Theses* to the door of the church, he embodied the iconic practice of freedom of speech. When he published the Bible in German, he enacted for all the world freedom of the press. And in leveling the hierarchy of the Church and the feudal estates of which it was an integral part, and replacing them with the "priesthood of all believers," he signaled the rise of republican government with its basis of authority, not in a king or a pope, but in the broad masses of individual citizens.

Luther was an intractable medievalist, looking backward for a simpler world that could never be revived. His Protest shattered the religious unity that had held Europe together for a thousand years. It would take three more centuries to come to full fruition, but out of the disparate pieces of culture that fell in his wake, the modern world was born.

10 Timeline

1453   Fall of Constantinople to Ottoman Turks

1455   Guttenberg invents the printing press in
            Mainz, Germany

1517   Luther posts *Ninety-Five Theses* on door of
            Wittenberg cathedral

1519   Luther denies papal infallibility in a
            debate with the Pope's emissary, Eck

1520   Luther is summoned to Rome to be tried
            for Heresy; Writes *An Open Letter to the
            Christian Nobility of the German Nation* urging
            German princes to reject Rome; Writes *On
            the Babylonian Captivity of the Church* denying
            the validity of the Sacraments

1521   Luther is formally excommunicated and
            banished from the Church

1522   Publishes first translation of *New Testament*
            in the local language, German

1531	Confession of Augsburg: Lutherans try to prove Biblical basis for their beliefs; Schmalkaldic League (mutual assistance among Protestant German princes) forms
1535	Henry VIII of England rejects papal authority; forms Church of England
1536	John Calvin writes *The Institutes of the Christian Religion*; Luther publishes first translation of Old Testament in German
1545	Council of Trent begins Catholic Reformation
1546	Luther dies; Schmalkaldic War between Catholic Holy Roman Empire and Protestant German princes
1552	Beginning of French Wars of Religion: Catholics vs. Huguenots (Calvinists)
1555	Peace of Augsburg: German princes determine religion within their own domains
1556	Beginning of the Dutch Revolt: Protestant Dutch vs. Catholic Spain
1559	Chateau Cambresis: Catholic French (Valois) and Spanish (Hapsburg) dynasties put aside differences to defeat common enemy: Protestantism

1598   Edict of Nantes ends French Wars of Religion: French equivalent to German Augsburg

1607   Jamestown founded by Protestants seeking religious freedom in the New World

1618   Beginning of the Thirty Years War: Catholics vs. Protestants in Germany

1642   Beginning of English Civil Wars: Anglicans vs. Puritans

1648   Peace of Westphalia ends Thirty Years War; establishes international law and the legal foundations of the modern nation state

1689   Glorious Revolution establishes world's first constitutional monarchy and affirms Protestant Church of England as official state church

1791   U.S. Bill of Rights ratified; separation of church and state enshrined in First Amendment to U.S. Constitution

If you enjoyed this book, please look for all of the titles in *The Best One-Hour History* series.

- Ancient Greece
- Rome
- The Middle Ages
- The Renaissance
- The Protestant Reformation
- European Wars of Religion
- The English Civil Wars
- The Scientific Revolution
- The Enlightenment
- The American Revolution
- The French Revolution
- The Industrial Revolution
- Europe in the 1800s
- The American Civil War
- European Imperialism
- World War I
- The Interwar Years
- World War II
- The Cold War
- The Vietnam War

To learn more about each title and its expected publication date, visit: *http://onehourhistory.com*

Printed in Great Britain
by Amazon.co.uk, Ltd.,
Marston Gate.